T0194253

The *Uncherished* *Wife*

Recover from the Emotionally Absent Man

BY

CHRISTINA VAZQUEZ

BALBOA.
PRESS

A DIVISION OF HAY HOUSE

Balboa Press books may be ordered through booksellers or by contacting:

Balboa Press
A Division of Hay House
1663 Liberty Drive
Bloomington, IN 47403
www.balboapress.com
1 (877) 407-4847

Because of the dynamic nature of the Internet, any web addresses or links contained in this book may have changed since publication and may no longer be valid. The views expressed in this work are solely those of the author and do not necessarily reflect the views of the publisher, and the publisher hereby disclaims any responsibility for them.

The author of this book does not dispense medical advice or prescribe the use of any technique as a form of treatment for physical, emotional, or medical problems without the advice of a physician, either directly or indirectly. The intent of the author is only to offer information of a general nature to help you in your quest for emotional and spiritual well-being. In the event you use any of the information in this book for yourself, which is your constitutional right, the author and the publisher assume no responsibility for your actions.

Any people depicted in stock imagery provided by Getty Images are models, and such images are being used for illustrative purposes only.
Certain stock imagery © Getty Images.

Print information available on the last page.

ISBN: 978-1-9822-1099-1 (sc)
ISBN: 978-1-9822-1101-1 (hc)
ISBN: 978-1-9822-1100-4 (e)

Library of Congress Control Number: 2018910153

Balboa Press rev. date: 09/18/2018

Contents

To my mother Michaelina with endless love,
whose steady encouragement gave me courage
to travel the road less traveled….

"No one can make you feel inferior without your consent."
Eleanor Roosevelt

CHAPTER ONE

Introduction

"Your heart knows things that your mind can't explain"
                                                    –Unknown

Let's be honest. Brutally honest. I mean in-your-face *courageous* honest. The kind of honest that pierces the heart and moves us to change. We've bought into the Illusion. Yep, from fiction novels to media – and for most of us, our parents or caretakers – a template, per se. A process to follow to be happy. An antiquated model that truly no longer serves us well. We've been conditioned to believe there is some perfect formula to happiness ... unconsciously most of us blindly believed our well-meaning "authorities." There are no absolutes when it comes to fulfillment – only preferences. That, in my world, is what we call conditioning. You see the only reason we believe what will make us happy is because somewhere along the line of our development it was implanted in us by some form of authority. Authority comes in many forms: parents, religion, culture, media, etc. Case in point – if from birth we had been told go up to the mountains, live in a cave, and need no one, then we would have believed *that* would bring us happiness in life. Make sense? We only know or believe by what has been programed into us. It's no different than a computer. Wipe the computer and put in new software and voila! New beliefs! That's simply all it is.

So each one of us steps into life with a set of beliefs about relationships that we are told will bring us lasting happiness. Until ... it doesn't. Very cerebral. So what got lost along the way? The small quiet voice within us did. Whether you call it Heart, God, Spirit, or intuition, it's not cerebral.

So this book will be a passageway back to where you once left that part of you behind. My dearest, you either were blatantly told to dismiss it, to not trust it, or it was implied that it doesn't exist. The sad thing is that on my journey to find it again within myself, I found it was this voice I suppressed – especially in the big decisions in life, i.e. marriage. Of course this whisper within would behoove us in all decisions in life, big or small, but most certainly in the life-altering ones!

So my goal here is to help you rediscover this voice within as we navigate through the struggles of your most significant and important relationship in life: marriage. Why? Why is it so important to access that part of ourselves in this relationship? Because it is without a shadow of doubt effects all other areas of your life and if we approach it too cerebrally, our heart will eventually catch up – and you will find yourself telling yourself some *story* or lie to keep convincing yourself that you are happy. You see dear one, *the mind is where the soul goes to hide from the heart.* The mind can tell us whatever we need to hear to keep us from looking at the truth of our hearts.

It takes courage, real courage to get 100 percent honest with our self. Not even 95 percent is good enough to be hard-core honest with ourselves. And I absolutely know you have the courage within you to get to that level of honesty with how you are feeling in your marriage and, more importantly, about yourself within the marriage. Trust me! I've been there ... it' takes guts to face the truth of our hearts head on, but by Design, we are more than given the tools to stand in front of the mirror and see reality. I was that confused woman who could not decipher what was true for me and what wasn't – sitting in a dark hole without a compass. It's a dark, heavy, scary place, but I am here to tell you there *is* a way to unveil the truth of your heart. I am honored to walk you through this exhilarating journey. Together, we'll explore every woman's desire to be cherished by her partner so much that she develops herself into finding her true purpose. It's a very different way of looking at marriage than either the religious traditional model or the "each man for himself" modern style. I came to discover that I had that desire to be not only loved but cherished by my father as a child and later, a husband, too. It was quite the journey for me to discover that it was this missing piece in my soul that left me feeling crazy at times. And that it does not need to be this way.

This is why I was compelled to write this book – so other women do not have to question themselves over and over and over and over when the "illusion" of the perfect husband still just "doesn't feel right." So women don't have to keep feeling they are out of their minds for not being happy with the 4000 sq. ft. custom home, the vacations, the cushy lifestyle, the cars, upscale dinners, and jewels. Asking themselves, "Am I loved? I guess? I mean I suppose by conventional standards. I mean isn't that what is *implied*?" Especially by our conditioning.

As a professional in the field of personal development, I am consistently astonished how little people know about relationships but even more so about themselves! Many of my clients are very educated – professionals from doctors to engineers – and yet in the area of emotional needs they are almost clueless! They are often so disconnected from themselves that when asked what they need or want in their marriage, they can't pinpoint it, at least on an emotional level. I do not say this with judgment but more with sadness that people have such minimal insight or awareness on this topic. They seem to lack the ability to connect how a relationship that makes a person feel that they are not only loved, but cherished down to the core, can determine if they are surviving or thriving.

Anthony Robbins, personal development expert and guru, brilliantly developed a model of the Six Core Human Needs. I will be referring to this model periodically throughout this book, since I have found it to be a very accurate assessment tool for why a marriage is either thriving or just surviving. For centuries, we have used a very cerebral or left-brained system to determine who we will unite with.... Seriously? I hope we are beyond picking a life partner like we are buying a car or home! I hear things like, "He comes from a nice family," "He helps a lot around the house," "He's good in the bedroom," "He's highly educated," or "He's financially successful." Of course all these qualities are duly noted in a relationship, but they are not the qualities that keep a relationship thriving and alive. And if we want the relationship to sustain the challenges that it undoubtedly brings, they should not be the primary factors in whether we enter or stay in marriage.

The *truth is* without our core needs being met at a highly satisfactory level, we as emotional beings will feel our inner spirit die. I experienced it as my light inside beginning to die. You see, one of the definitions I found of the word cherish is to "cultivate with care." Cultivate? Grow or prepare? Grow or prepare for what? For whatever we are here to do! For all we are meant to be! I, with every cell of my being, believe this is the Truth of what the sacred contract of marriage was intended for. It is in the energy of being cherished that we flourish into a way of being that serves us and our world for all's highest good, living at our highest potential.

We are living, breathing beings with *real* emotional needs. These needs are not some air-fairy idealistic want. They are bona fide needs to survive with the potential to thrive! It took me decades to come to this realization. Now I want to share it with you.

I will elaborate more on my journey in the next chapter but for now let me familiarize you with what these six needs are:

Personality Needs
- Certainty
- Variety
- Love/Connection
- Significance

Spirit Needs
- Growth
- Contribution

The reality is you will get these needs met one way or another. Let me reemphasize. These are not optional needs; they are *survival* needs for human beings, like food and water. So much that we may even find ourselves compromising our value system to get them met. As a therapist, I have worked with numerous clients who in their wildest dreams would never have stepped out of their marriage for love, connection, or significance yet often, when the need for connection or significance was met near zero within the relationship on a scale from 1-10, they found themselves quite vulnerable to infidelity – if not physically, most certainly emotionally.

Infidelity is not the only way to exit a marriage emotionally. Consider the workaholic husband who spends countless hours in the work place. Could it be his job is demanding? Absolutely. But it is often where men – and women as well within our modern society – get a high level of significance/appreciation. Or the woman who is involved in every philanthropic group in the community to meet her desperate need for connection when hubby is emotionally checked out. Do you see now how whether we are aware of it or not, we are getting our emotional needs met somewhere?

A couple things here are key factors. To me, the first one is: consciously or unconsciously? In other words, are we *aware* where we get our emotional needs met? If not, this is how we can slip into compulsive behaviors or addictions of all sorts to *get* our needs met. They can be behavioral or physiological. Either way, the need is being primarily met outside the relationship therefore that is often where our time and energy is spent. This can leave the wife of the well-meaning workaholic feeling completely uncherished yet also feeling the dissonance by intellectualizing his love in observing his "justified" hard work. What she sees and what she feels are in contradiction. If that isn't crazy in the making?

To cherish someone is a verb. It's an ongoing attitude and behavior that feeds the living, breathing organism of a relationship until physical death. Spiritually, the emotional death of a marriage is when the marriage truly ends. Apathy has set in and the desire to "tend to," uphold, and revere your partner is gone. There could be dozens of reasons it got there but the reality is…. It is.

Now comes the choice: to co-create into a partnership that cherishes one another in the true sense of the word or to discern if the relationship has moved toward a place of contempt which research has proven to be cancer to a marriage.

As Anthony Robbins asks, in the *Six Core Needs*, "Are we getting this need met in a positive form, negative (destructive form), or a neutral form?"

As we grow and become more conscious of these emotions as *needs*, we can be more deliberate in choosing how we get them met. It is when we unconsciously choose self-destructive or relationship-shattering behaviors that we are meeting them in a negative form.

The easiest way to discern whether it is negative is to ask yourself the question: "Will this behavior make my partner feel more cherished, less cherished, or have no impact either way?"

This single question can bring clarity to whether a behavior or direction we choose will bring us closer to our desired outcome, in this case strengthen the bond, or have no significance.

So what I am trying to point out here is: If you continue to evaluate your relationship in a cerebral manner, you may find yourself in a bit of a quandary or even a place of shame for not being grateful for what "appears" to be the ideal life. My negative self-talk was brutal during this stage! For a long time, I made certain decisions or evaluations in my life from a survival mode. I was completely ignoring the fact that I primarily am a spiritual and emotional being. Again, much of these thought processes were coming from my early conditioning that I integrated as an absolute. Only later did I learn to discover the root of my emotional thirst within the relationship by evaluating through a more tangible method what the deficits were for me in my marriage.

To our detriment, most of us have been conditioned to make one of our most vital choices in life way too intellectually – as though we are empty shells of matter versus heart-centered creatures. Every day, within my practice, I see women waking up to this truth in themselves. They know they feel lonely … unseen and uncherished in their marriage but are confused as to why. Women can intellectually say "I have a good life," but yet cannot seem to quite name that missing piece. Not feeling love for me was a bit easier to recognize. Slightly more identifiable. But being cherished by someone is a whole different feeling. Sadly, most of us said those words to another at the altar and yet truly had no clue what they meant when vowed. Wanting to be cherished was a hidden desire within me buried by the noise of a chattering ego mind.

It's been quite a journey to rediscover that early inner knowing I once had and take its voice very seriously. Be relentless and determined if you are set on finding that voice again. I promise you it is within reach and most certainly worth the energy devoted to the process. I am honored to facilitate this journey back to You.

CHAPTER TWO

My Story

"Nothing in life is to be feared, it is only to be understood. Now is the time to understand more, so that we may fear less."

–Marie Curie

I have always been a highly sensitive person. Growing up, it was commonplace for my mother or siblings to call me too sensitive or a crybaby. I began to feel shame about myself. What was wrong with me that I felt emotion so deeply while others seemed to let it roll off them? Born in the 60s, I remember I could not get through the credits and closing song of *Lassie* without crying. At that time I felt pathetic – now I look fondly back on the young girl and see the beauty of her heart and smile. As I did "my work," I came to see that part of me as my true essence – how God made me in Perfect Design. Through my experience of being raised by a mother who was quite out of touch with her feelings and did not validate my feelings but minimized them due to her own repression of emotion, I believed within myself that feelings were not real, often saying to myself "I guess maybe I don't feel (sad, angry, hurt) – it's just that I'm too thin-skinned." My mother was a very devoted Catholic woman. A wonderful, kind woman – but, in order to deal with her own struggles, she either intellectualized her pain or did the spiritual bypass. As I grew older, and got myself into therapy, I would challenge her on her emotions. But her reply was always the same. "Jesus is enough." I am extremely grateful from a spiritual perspective she modeled to me – for in my own challenges, my faith has served me greatly – but I could not ignore the fact we are emotional beings as well.

It took me a long time to get what it means to feel and be in your body at the same time. So the only way I knew how to survive my overwhelming emotion was to intellectualize, minimize, or – in essence – lie to myself about what I was feeling. For much of my life, I lived what I now know as an unconscious protective stance. For as long as I can remember, I have been on a search mission to find, "What the hell is wrong with me? I feel so different from everyone else. I don't fit in." Again, I cannot tell you the thousands of times I said those words to myself. Brutal judgment. If any of this is resonating with you, which I have a hunch it is if you were drawn to this book, I encourage you to do self-study on empaths. There is tons of information on the internet. I also recommend an excellent book by Ora North called *I Don't Want to Be an Empath Anymore*. If you believe you may be one, it would benefit you to understand it more.

Circling back now to my story: My marriage took me on a journey that felt like self-destruction, depression, and near death in my spirit.

My story for that era was quite typical. As a product of the 60s and 70s, my path to a "good life" was pretty well mapped out. My father was born in Puerto Rico and moved to the states to attend DePaul University, eventually to become an attorney. My home was very traditional. My mother stayed home to raise her five kids, with myself being the youngest. She never finished college, never learned to drive, or never held a job. She was the proverbial barefoot and pregnant woman whose life purpose was to serve her husband and children. We lived in an upper-middle-class neighborhood in a southwest suburb of Chicago. This model was pretty typical for that era except for my mother's inability to drive or to have any access to money. It was my normal to see her receive her $10 allowance and depend on my father for near everything. The only independence I witnessed was her walking to church every single Sunday, devotedly, without fail.

As a therapist, near 50 percent of my clientele is couples. In their initial session, one of the first assessment questions I ask them is what was their model growing up of a marriage: a significant question in relationship work to determine attitudes and perspectives. Also, as a hypnotherapist, I know the imprints made on a child's psychological development under the age of five and especially during the preverbal years have a significant impact on the neuroplasticity of the brain. I'm not here to go into depth on this subject but feel free to do more of your own research on the that topic or the subconscious mind.

My parents' relationship was very tumultuous. A hot-headed, loud man who operated from a double standard in line with his culture and society married a proper, ladylike, Catholic to the core, and more even-tempered second generation Italian woman from Baltimore. Oil and water. Put five spirited *kids* in there and it was pure chaos!

This very patriarchal home was my model of marriage. I remember fantasizing in my grade school years as I would watch sitcoms like the Donna Reed Show (60s) to the Brady Bunch (70s). It seemed as though my sole life ambition was to find a good, quiet man, have children and live happily ever after. The confusing part at time though is that my father gave me and my two sisters mixed messages. He married a submissive woman who he dominated while pushing us to get a college education so we would not be dependent on a man. As I moved toward the college years, I felt I absorbed the first message unconsciously and the latter more consciously.

Just before the first semester of my sophomore year, I met a very good looking frat boy who on campus was known as a bit "wild" but also seemingly shy. His affect seemed super chill and very non-reactive which was extremely appealing to me after being raised by an angry father who scared the bejesus out of me daily. So as fate would have it, we began to date and were almost inseparable the first year. Rick was also from a very traditional home but opposite of mine in that it was not chaotic. They were a staunch Polish family, highly refined and somewhat well-to-do. I mean they actually all sat down quietly together every night and ate dinner civilly! Wow! What a contrast from mine. This was very appealing to me as a young college girl because in my mind, it was the way a family "should" be.

We continued to date through my undergrad years and got engaged just short of my graduation. He had many of the – what I believed to be – "good husband" qualities. From my blueprint, Rick represented the epitome of security – everything I believed would keep me safe in the world. My own father became more and more absent as my parents' marriage deteriorated. Rick, to me, was everything my dad wasn't. He would never abandon me the way I felt my father had continually....at least not *physically*, not even close to be aware of at the young age of 22 that emotional abandonment was possible. No, I did not feel with him like I believed a bride was supposed to on her wedding day but I did feel secure and safe. Rick was solid. A good family man, hard worker, attractive and from a good home. As the wedding grew closer, everything in my body was telling me *no* but I thought it was usual commitment jitters. I mean afterall, he was a great catch of a spouse for my "blueprint" and he *seemed* to love me a lot. All the other core needs paled in comparison. To marry a man and live with a fear of abandonment for the rest of my life was terrifying! Rick was a safe choice. In retrospect, and as I have grown spiritually, I do realize in life we truly only make decisions from one of two places: fear or love. Fear won. Don't get me wrong – I loved Rick, still do, but my ability to discern what components were imperative to me in a life-long partner was defective because my heart was covered with fear. Whenever we make a decision from fear we are moving further from our authentic self. No doubt whatsoever that much good came out of my marriage – but also a lot of pain. I know one could argue that everything happens as "it should" and I agree with that. Pain is part of the human experience. It's inevitable. But there is pain that leads to growth and pain that can lead us further away from what we truly want.

Fear blocks Truth. We lose clarity, focus, center, and perspective. The more we continue to make decisions in our life from fear, the further from our true north we go. It's never too late to find your way back. Never. Not as long as you are breathing.

Being raised a strong Catholic, divorce never felt like an option. Guilt. Good ol' Catholic guilt. Another useless emotion that takes us off center. "I made a vow before God so I *have* to make this marriage work." I had to not only stay with it but also make sure I "looked" like I was thriving in it. What would people think of the so called perfect little white suburban family? The shame. The judgment!

Rick was hired as a state policeman literally the week we got married. The day after we returned from our honeymoon he took off for 16 weeks of training at the police academy to start his lifelong career as a police officer. He would drive home for a day-and-a-half visit on the weekends, which helped with some of loneliness I would experience as a young wife.

When he returned from training, Rick continued his career as a police officer. I had entered the field of retail management after college, so coinciding schedules were few and far between. Holidays too were erratic.

In retrospect, the only reason I think I was okay with the loneliness was because it was normal for me. Being the youngest of five kids – and the last to leave for college – it was just me and my mom for many years since my dad was rarely home until the marriage disintegrated when I was 17. It was not an ideal way to start a marriage but it was a familiar way of existing. I'm an introvert so I really can enjoy my own company for hours but this feeling went way beyond that need to be alone. I didn't even feel "married."

Rick was not a big conversationalist and certainly not expressive. Ideal personality for a cop. We could go out to dinner, even as a young couple, and I easily would do 80 percent of the talking or we could spend time at home together having very little conversation or interaction. I played wife, he played husband. It still was secure and stable.

Rick and I went on to have three beautiful daughters. I loved being a mom. Still do. It felt very natural to me. I felt "at home" with my role. It was challenging but in the good kind of way in that the pros completely outweighed the cons. Besides, with hubby gone so much, my daughters were wonderful company. We got to do all the girly things together and it was very fulfilling. I didn't realize it then but it was filling all the gaps in my heart in a pseudo manner.

I continued to work *very* hard (probably too hard) to create this perfect scenario of a life I thought would protect me from having to feel whatever I didn't want to feel or face. In some ways, it served to do that when I chose to stay in "my illusion." But as the years went on, a voice kept getting increasingly louder inside. Rick and

I used a variety of coping mechanisms to escape our hearts' truth. Some personally destructive, some not so personally destructive.

In my world, I call these addictions. Just being honest. We are all addicts. It's a spectrum. An addiction is no more than a conscious or unconscious choice to disconnect from our self (or the truth of our hearts) and/or from others. It can range from joining every philanthropic organization in the community to drugs, sex, alcohol or even television. It's all an escape or an avoidance from being honest with ourselves. Truly honest. Why? Because if we got truly honest with our heart, the angst would continue to grow so greatly until we had to do something about it or we'd go mad.

So this was my struggle. My plight. My conundrum. Finding 10,000 ways to avoid the truth of my heart. Back then, the reality is I really "thought" I was being honest with myself. I mean, what more could I have wanted? I had it all. Living the American Dream. The illusion. But then why did I feel so dead inside? I continued to grow in my spirituality, personal development, and career goals but that nagging angst of emptiness was still there and if anything, growing stronger.

It was about this time that I knew what was missing was an alive connection in my marriage. I longed – and I mean longed – for real connection, passion, desire. I wanted to be seen. I judged myself brutally for wanting it. Why did all the other women around me seem perfectly content in their lives? What was wrong with me?

I knew through years of therapy that it was not at all uncommon for women from homes of an absent father, either physically or emotionally, to seek male attention. It was something consciously I was aware of, but as a married woman, struggled to avoid. But being honest with myself, I yearned for "love". In retrospect, because I did not know how to love myself first. So unfortunately, I allowed myself to receive it outside the marriage even though it was in a shallow form. Perfect example of a destructive way of getting a need met.

Back to more therapy (couples and individual). Even couples' retreats. The angst would subside for a while, but then seemed to come back stronger. Something in spite of the therapy and growth was still awry. Again years later the perfect storm emerged: magnetized into another affair. This time it felt overwhelmingly all-consuming. It had been so long since I felt this alive. Of course not the wisest of choices but at that time almost felt like emotional *survival*. Undoubtedly, I was still struggling to value and cherish myself, which was only exacerbated by my behavior. Nor did I seem to have the ability to communicate to my spouse what I needed from him. *Or* was it just that he was *unable* to feel or had no concept of how to go deeper in the relationship but could not verbalize or identify it for himself?

Regardless, all of that led to nowhere good, just to more pain. And I mean pain. The structure of the marriage remained intact or at least the "illusion" of it because neither one of us was able to own the truth of our hearts. So I pulled myself together and returned to telling myself all the reasons I "should" be happy with my life. At last, I finally was able to quell my restless heart – for a few years.

Then circumstances were serendipitously brought about in a way that I knew I could no longer hide from the truth of my heart. God was making it clear to me that if I ever wanted to heal my heart and listen to my soul, things in my life were going to have to get mighty real. So I put on my big girl pants, made a commitment to myself that I would no longer betray myself by ignoring the voice within, and began the journey of *true* transformation.

CHAPTER THREE

Trance to Transformation

"If we only see things through the cold-eyed lens of factuality and don't listen to the yearning and screaming of unexpressed feelings, life may remain bleak in a mire of clinical hollowness, sodden in apathy and indifference."

—Erik Pevernagie

Moving through the process of de-conditioning and clearing away all the "programing" we have encountered from birth (actually from the womb) takes commitment. Commitment not only to the process but to oneself. In this book, I take you through the steps that are necessary to uncovering the quiet inner voice within. Call it what you will … your heart, Truth, God, Higher Self, Soul, or what have you. You will "know" it when you find it. You will *feel* it.

Unfortunately, most of us have lost the art of listening to this voice through our conditioning but I assure you, it is there. It was and always will be. I could make this complicated and recommend years of therapy to uncover it but it really doesn't have to be that hard. Remember, we are always choosing from two emotions, always moving toward love or fear. It can be that simple but for most of us it takes some clearing and practice … just like any new discipline.

So go back to the original point of you even picking up this book. You are in a quandary. By the world's standards, you should feel happy and loved. You have situated your life "on the outside" to line up in your head. You *should* be happy. Then why aren't you? What is that je ne sais quoi that is not there? In theory, you have many of the good components of a decent relationship; don't argue that much, comfortable in many ways and overall there are no *major* issues. Actually, you pretty much get to do what you please in the day-to-day things. Sound pretty accurate? Sounds like a pretty ideal life to me!

Except for one thing. The relationship is flat. It feels dead. There's love, so to speak, but something is missing.

In my experience, personally and professionally, most people are completely satisfied with a marriage that operates at this level. It's functional. It's not bad but not great. It's safe and familiar. But what is missing? We know that a certain love exists so why do we want more?

It's about this time that your mother, sister, or BF says, "What do you expect? You are not in the honeymoon phase anymore!"

Which yes, typically dissipates any from 12 -18 months … although it does not have to … nor do I believe a thriving relationship is absent of that je ne sais quoi. But if in your heart, that you so desperately want more – like I did – you want your relationship to feel alive and growing – then my words will speak to you. That desire is not there due to ingratitude, selfishness, or anything of the ilk but by Design. It's what keeps the relationship alive. You are not cray-cray for desiring it!

Before I was in the business of personal development, I had a part-time career in the fitness industry. Besides instructing classes, I was a personal trainer. The majority of my clients know I parallel the physical body with the emotional body quite often. I find transformation on either level happens when change is not optional for us. When we decide we are done living, being or *acting* a certain way – once and for all that is dictated more from our conditioning than what "feels" in alignment to our heart. The pain is intolerable and we must find a way out of it. This is what I call a motivated client, both in my current career and former. I love these clients because, like myself, they will do whatever it takes for change to take place. It took me a seriously long time to realize that if *nothing changes, nothing changes.* I had to get tired approaching a problem the same way and expecting things to be different. Time and again, clients would return to me year after year hitting the same wall because they just weren't ready to be honest with themselves. But I don't judge their journey, one, because I get it (been there) and two, because it's part of the road to transformation. Some people have to circle the block once, some circle dozens of times, and sadly for some, they never wake up but stay on the merry-go-round. At least that ride is familiar. We find comfort in familiarity even if it's painful. We are amazing creatures that way.

So for the rest of this book, I will share with you the process toward true transformation. The *only* prerequisite you need to have is to want it with all your heart and soul. Then, my friend, you will get there.

There is freedom in living authentically to one's true nature. I personally am ecstatic to be here and want the same for you. You discover amazing things about life, yourself, and others along this path. You may even find yourself experiencing things in this lifetime you never thought you would. I did. And I hope the same for you.

In the beginning of this book, I mentioned that either due to our conditioning or emotional sensitivity levels, we have learned or become more comfortable with approaching decisions in life, often major ones, from a very cerebral method.

Clearly most decisions should involve aspects of both logic and emotion, but I have personally found when we are able to hear the voice of our "inner knowing" that voice will always lead us to a place of growth or expansion. How exciting! Yep, I am in that minority of people that thrives on change!

I'm pretty sure you have a good sense of how to view your relationship from a logical point of view. The process I am going to take you through in these next chapters will aid you in bringing forth your intuitive side. I want you to learn how to trust the sensations in your body. We are aware when we are feeling an emotion, at least if we're honest with ourselves. But are you conscious? I mean really conscious, of the sensations in your body that also coincide with the emotions?

We are multi-dimensional beings. The body is *always* in communication with us. Consistently giving us clues or trying to get our attention. The problem is we so often are checked out or oblivious to it that we blow past the signals. Until we can't. Panic attacks, depression, disease, or even cancer. Even a stubbed toe can be a message to slow down or watch where you are going. We are constantly being guided, directed, or spoken to if we stay present in life.

If you are an HSP (or an empath) but have not really understood it or learned how to discern or work with your sensitivities, then this process will guide you to trusting yourself more. If you lean toward approaching your emotions from a more logical perspective, then I will share with you processes that can help you clear the barriers or protective layers that keep you from accessing your true heart.

Once you really get in tune with your body you will see how all along you had so many of the answers you were looking for on the way. "You've always had the power my dear, you just had to learn it for yourself." (Glinda, *The Wizard of Oz*)

CHAPTER FOUR

Listen to Your Heart

"The best and most beautiful things in the world cannot be seen or even touched - they must be felt with the heart."

–Helen Keller

When it comes to matters of the heart the information can be quite conflicting. From religion to science, we may have been told by "authorities" multiple messages about whether to heed or dismiss our heart. Inherently, because I am person who feels deeply, which can be a blessing or a curse, I have struggled greatly in trusting my heart. The more I have learned and practiced feeling truth in my body, the more I recognize it and trust it.

The HeartMath Institute, a nonprofit founded in 1991, states that their research "is to help people bring their physical, mental, and emotional systems into balanced alignment with their heart's intuitive guidance." I am ecstatic that there is now science-based evidence on the information sent between the heart and the brain. The research at HeartMath shows the heart plays a greater role in our mental, emotional, and physical processes than we once believed. HeartMath studies have shown that the heart generates the largest electromagnetic field in the body – 60 times greater than the brain. The heart actually sends more signals to the brain than the brain sends to the heart. So why is this information so valuable? For me, it validated that much of what I had felt in my emotions or body since childhood is not just "in my head" or "silly notions!" My body was trying to get my attention. Often I felt it, but too often, I intellectualized it away. Don't get me wrong – there is "a place" for intellect in our decision making – but discernment is key.

So what does it mean to feel truth in our body? First, let me define what I mean by truth. In this book I do not mean it as an absolute or moral truth universally. I'm saying "truth" is what is the best direction given what I've experienced, the lessons I consciously choose to learn, and the experiences I consciously desire to have. I do believe if we listen to our truth, we are ultimately being divinely led on our life path, even if to others it may look contrary. I have come to understand that if we listen to that inner voice in our bodies – even if the circumstances may look absurd or against others' beliefs – there is something within us that points us in a certain direction for our growth and evolution.

Deciding to leave a marriage is not an easy decision. There are many factors that were involved in my decision. I was constantly looking for a crystal-clear answer – mostly from God. Due to my strong Christian background, I was tortured daily with guilt. "God hates divorce," the Bible says. In my practice, I deal with divorce consistently and certainly see the pain divorce brings to individuals and children, no matter what age. My strong religious conditioning – mixed with concerns of judgment of close family and friends who had come to see me in a certain light – plagued me daily.

I was torn apart inside about hurting a man I had known for over three decades and had gone through many life experiences with. The love was dutifully there but that small voice within – the pull within my body – was telling me it was time to let go. The relationship had withered. It felt like it was being held together by scotch tape. We were no longer becoming better versions of our true selves but the exact opposite. The relationship felt heavy ... energetically like a gravitational force holding us from moving into our later years in life with excitement, energy, passion, and purpose. I could literally feel it in my body.

As a hypnotherapist, heart-centered hypnotherapy is an effective process I've used with clients to gain clarity with an issue they are struggling with. "How does this feel in your body?" is repeatedly asked to my client in their meditative state. When we are able to be present and go inward to listen to what our body is trying to communicate answers can be found. Often with much clarity.

It's quite a simple process that can be done easily when we *create* the space. So do it! Create the space in your day consistently. Commit to hearing from within.

Simply quiet yourself through breathing or soothing music. Place your hand on your solar plexus and ask a question. Breathe and allow the answer to come into your mind. Trust me and stay focused on your breath. You will feel the resonance in your body to the answer or idea that came up for you as you are being guided toward *your* truth.

I worked with a client the other day to explore her feelings around her marriage. Consciously, she had circled round and round what was "missing" in her life. I instructed her to close her eyes and lie still, and breathe into the area of her body that was responding to the question – in this case it was her chest (or heart space). As I asked the question, and she patiently waited for the inner voice to answer, she was able to identify the piece. The tears came as she saw the truth of what she wanted from her marriage. She now had the clear information to go to her husband and ask for what she desired. They now as a couple had a tangible, identifiable piece to work with toward creating a more satisfying relationship.

Carl Jung introduced a concept called "synchronicity" in the 1920s. One of the definitions Wikipedia gives is a "meaningful coincidence" or a more accurate description is a significant coincidence where physical and psychological factors are related by meaning.

Determined to have clarity on my decision to divorce, I became hyper-vigilant to synchronicity in my life.

I'm not a huge follower on Pinterest but here and there peruse it for creative ideas on a variety of topics. One day I came across a meme, "The Body Doesn't Lie." Whoa!

That was a *yes* moment for me! I knew it! There was synchronicity affirming that listening to my body was a viable method of gaining clarity on whether to leave my marriage or not. The more I thought about it the more it made sense. How could the body lie? It's an objective form of feedback – meaning like our personal, God-given "lie detector."

Another method I stumbled across in my learning was asking yourself whether something in your life feels heavy or light. For example, if you're trying to decide whether to leave your job or not. Sit quietly for a few minutes, close your eyes, and ask yourself, "If I were to leave this job tomorrow would that feel heavier or lighter in my life?" "If I were to move to a different home would that feel heavier or lighter?" Sometimes, just sitting with our eyes closed quietly for a few moments we can feel whether something is weighing us down in our life or freeing us up to align with our authentic self. I got this simple little exercise from listening to a motivational speaker called Kyle Cease. Check him out sometime on YouTube – he's a great presenter and absolutely hysterical!

Speaking of the term alignment, I did a short presentation a few years back at my chiropractor's office. I called it "Emotional Alignment." I came up with that title because, occasionally during my visits to my chiropractor, he would often educate me on the importance of having spinal alignment so the body can heal. Made sense to me. How can a hose have a full stream of water running through it if there are bends in it, right? Again, as I began to parallel that to the emotional body, I realized if we have subluxations or kinks within our emotional system, then we will not be able to: one, heal and two, to have a clear path to what is true for us. I began to ponder this analogy more and how this also applied to the emotional system. I came to an awareness, that I love to share with my clients who are a bit newer to the self-help world. If there were blockages in our intestinal tract and we could not eliminate waste from our body, we would literally die! God in his infinite wisdom designed our emotional bodies to work exactly the same way.

I have found if we do not clear the heavy emotions or negativity we carry in our body, we feel heavy and sluggish. This is why it's imperative to take time to sit quietly and go within and feel for what feels heavy in our life or what is blocking our emotional energy from flowing. This method has been invaluable to me in my process of discerning what is in alignment with my life path and purpose.

The heart. The heart. The heart. The heart. Sometimes I get so frustrated living in a world that predominately functions from such a cerebral perspective! Aaaaaaaaaaargh! I mean, I get it. But our nature is not cerebral. We are spiritual beings having a human experience. If you're in the spiritual world, I'm saying nothing you haven't heard. But let me reemphasize: We are spiritual beings having a human experience. Period. Not the other way around. Until this world fully absorbs that truth and operates from this higher perspective, we will always hit struggle. Spirit flows. Ego separates and compartmentalizes.

Circling back to my original point: Near everything of serious consequence in life, is driven by our heart, whether you recognize it or not. Nearly twenty years ago, when I was working on my master's degree in counseling from a very academic Christian University, I studied the Bible in depth. Even though I have expanded quite a bit in my spiritual thinking since then, I have never lost many of the spiritual truths of that journey.

Funny but most of the verses that pierced me – with that same physiological sensation I referred to earlier – were verses that pertained to the heart. The one I repeated over and over to myself when I dropped into that non-productive feeling of feeling judged or criticized by certain self-righteous people is from 1 Samuel in the Old Testament. "Man (ego) looks on the outward appearance but God looks at the heart." (spirit) (paraphrased).

So with that said, I come to my last very crucial factor in this chapter about the heart. This one I struggled greatly with as I deliberated and deliberated over leaving my marriage. I am going to flip over to my clinical side here as a therapist but promise you I will tie it to the spiritual. Love it! (One of my favorite pastimes: finding the commonality of religion and science ;-)) The term is codependency. Almost all people I know hear this and think "I am not a codependent. How can I be when my partner is not an addict?" They are usually thinking of addiction in terms of substance abuse or a behavioral addiction like sex or gambling. Nope, not true. Somewhere along my training in heart-centered hypnotherapy from the Wellness Institute in Seattle, one of my outstanding instructors referred to codependency as emotional dishonesty. Bingo! There was that feeling of truth in my body. Prior to that I kind of, sort of, thought I was codependent. My ex was an on-and-off binge drinker often intertwined with less than desirable behavior that I intermittently dealt with over the course of our marriage but I was working on my boundaries with it so I really was not *that* codependent. Oh, how we deceive ourselves. The lie I had to keep on telling myself to make believe I was okay with things. *Ugh.* But these words "emotional dishonesty" pierced me. Again, more words of Jesus paraphrased: truth is alive and powerful … cutting between soul and spirit … discerning thoughts of the heart. I'd thought of dishonesty as downright lying, whether it was calling off work when you weren't truly sick or telling your mom you were somewhere else than where you said you were. You get it. Now I define emotional dishonesty for my clients as when your head is nodding yes and your heart is saying no, or vice versa. Maybe for some people that is a simple behavior to overcome but unfortunately the way I was conditioned in my childhood it was not. My well-meaning, subservient, good Catholic mom trained me well to be a people-pleaser or even more so, a man-pleaser. I won't go into detail of all ways that was modeled or taught to me but it was like shrapnel in my body. So the process of slowly teasing it out of my system had to be a very intentional and merciless process.

Once I was introduced to this form of codependency, it was acutely in my awareness.

I obsessively began to review my life for all the ways throughout It where I was living from this pattern. From eating dinner at a childhood friend's home and saying I loved liverwurst because her mother had made us sandwiches and not wanting to be "rude" but then proceeding to puke or to going along with behaviors or attitudes of my adult friends that were inherently against my values.

But no, it didn't stop there! My life and marriage were infected with it! I spent years suppressing my own wants and desires in hopes not to feel rejection. The years went on and I further slipped into this pattern not only in Rick's family, but with my own family of origin, with neighbors, community organizations, within the church I served in, and, most significantly, impacting my marriage. THIS was how I slowly lost myself over the decades.

As I continued to go along with things in my marriage that were not okay with me or in alignment with my true self, I found the relationship began to feel heavier and heavier.

You see codependency is also an addiction. Yup – an addiction to putting others' needs and desires before your own. Clearly there is nothing wrong with putting others before yourself at times. That is being a loving or kind person by choice, with no resentment in your heart. Healthy. But when it becomes so chronic that you start to lose yourself in the process and get so far from alignment of who you once were – that to me is very concerning. Why? Because there is no way you will ever feel whole – much less fulfill your life's true purpose.

There were many factors that led to my choice to divorce, but somewhere about halfway through my marriage is when I began to feel the inertia of this energy. My spiritual growth was taking me continually to new awarenesses and I could feel and often, in our conversations, knew Rick and I were on way different pages. I guess I could say he was very religious and I was becoming (maybe birthed from religion) more expansive spiritually. I truly believed Rick could not live life from his heart while I was learning to live more and more from my heart. Trust me, we had countless arguments, debates, and counseling sessions to try and find resonance. The reality was that if I was truly – and I mean truly – honest with the emptiness I was feeling, I would have to make a choice. A very hard choice. This was a brutal process for me. I was petrified to start over after all these years with Rick. Our marriage was comfortable, familiar, and very safe. I had built my whole life to create a world of safety for myself and my family. Well-meaning, yes; well-serving, not so much. It became increasingly clearer to me that building this "perfect" little life and not being "emotionally honest" was actually not serving anyone.

Since age three or four, I had known I was a spiritual little being. I felt connection to God and *knew* there was something more out there. So because I am known to analyze things to death (I just call it being a deep thinker), I was on a mission to align my spiritual path with my purpose and the truth of my heart. My strong Christian background left me in a gut-wrenching turmoil as I battled with the decision to stay or go. But what kept coming to me was "what is marriage?" So let's be honest here. As a baby boomer, my model was very societal. But this was no longer resonating with my heart. I started to think about how culturally, women – for the most part, from my generation and especially from more traditional families – were groomed to believe they needed a man to take care of them. Society was changing around me while my conditioning model was blatantly telling me the opposite. It became more and more obvious to me that I was in a marriage that I was intellectually choosing due to old beliefs from my primitive brain while my consciousness was moving forward. I was feeling dissonance … contradicting beliefs! As long as I was processing that way, I would never feel in alignment. So I begin to ponder more, "What truly is a marriage? Where does it take place?" A marriage is a conscious contract between two people that takes place in the heart.

Back to my theology. Jesus taught that whether we sin against another human being in our mind or in an action, energetically it is the same. I couldn't do it anymore. I was living a lie and it was holding me back on my spiritual path. Religion and rules were not going to change what was in my heart. Living in this dissonance was actually taking me further from the direction I wanted to go in life. I was compromising my values, I did not like who I was becoming, and I knew I could not live this way one more minute or I would spiritually die!

I remember going to Rick at various times toward the end of our marriage to try and openly discuss this issue. But it was evident our views were opposing. His more "religious," mine more spiritual. He thought I was nuts. The more I looked around me, whether in the church, my community, or even family, the more I saw people in shackles in their marriages. I saw it that many of us (not all) were bound by a contract made unconsciously at a much earlier time of life due to a variety of reasons.

Until I sat with it all in my heart. Everything in my body kept saying "move forward." Crazy as this may sound, when I really went within, I could almost feel a firm hand on my back pushing me forward and a gravitational pull in front of me. My reasons for going back all were tied to fear! I refused to give into it one more time in my life. Clearly, when I made decisions from fear, my self-worth was compromised, which created shame, which just kept me in a vicious whirlwind – and I wanted off. I wanted consciously to live my life as authentically as possible. Live out loud! Come clean to the world! Addiction? Maybe? But to what? Approval? Image? My need to keep my daughters "safe from life?" My need to be responsible for others' happiness while martyring my own? I had to free myself and by default, Rick, too. I was scared but so what – in my eyes, I had no choice. Fear is just "false evidence appearing real." So the quickest way to dispel that is to begin bringing to mind every situation you acted from your heart even though you were afraid and note the outcome. I promise you have a storehouse of them. Ego will present a case for the opposite but Spirit will always find evidence on your life's timeline that action, when directed from our inner voice, is moving to align us to our heart's desire.

Since my late twenties, I have wanted to live a life of purpose and influence and in many ways, I was doing it in integrity – until I wasn't. It wasn't fair to Rick or my daughters to continue living a lie.

I remember hearing somewhere during my separation that when we follow our soul's path, it bumps others into theirs. It completely resonated with me in a spiritual way. Aha! Codependency was the addiction that was making it impossible for me to move forward into the life I dreamed of on so many different levels. I realized breaking out of this man-made construct was my spiritual path to my life purpose and possibly Rick's and my daughters' if they so chose. Through every one of the processes I mentioned in this chapter, I was able to separate successfully my ego (fear) from spirit (love) – which has allowed me to create a life that reflects my authentic self.

When I take clients through these modalities – or they implement them on their own – they too are able to align their relationship to create what they are wanting from it or find the clarity they need to move on to something that cherishes their true self.

CHAPTER FIVE

Reality Check

"Love takes off masks that we fear we cannot live without and know we cannot live within."
—James Baldwin

So here you are in a tug of war with your head and your heart. I think one of my biggest objectives during my separation was to gain clarity. That can be quite challenging when deep-rooted conditioning (hind brain stuff) and your spirit are feeling pulled in opposite directions. Since I was trying to really "get this right" and not make an emotionally willy-nilly decision based on my desire to "feel loved" or "live my truth," I investigated the best relationship experts out there to see if I was missing something. Second guessing myself and needing to make sure I have turned every stone is also another lifelong pattern of mine.

All my defaults were kicking in. Remember, the longer you have been thinking or acting a certain way, the stronger the inertia or force to carry that thought pattern or belief forward. It's why cults prey on young weak minds — because they are most influential. Anyway, this is why change can be so hard for some people — because our mind, ego, brain wants to go back to what is *comfortable*. Doesn't necessarily mean it's right, healthy, or even in alignment with our heart. And God knows how us beings love to be comfortable!

When I coach my clients on a strategy to erase old or faulty "programing," I tell them the diligence and tenacity it can take to install new "programing." It is by practice and repetition that we create new beliefs that align better with the life we are desiring. Remember the adage, "Tell yourself a lie long enough and you begin to believe it?" If you work with me individually, I do have a couple shortcuts to reprogramming but it still takes committed diligence.

Back in the first chapter, I introduced you to a model called the *Six Core Human Needs* by Anthony Robbins. What I love about this model is that it puts the state of the relationship in more black and white terms. When I coach couples, the men particularly are able to "get" more on a head level why they are feeling the way they do within the marriage or partnership. This assessment is a wonderful baseline to note where the weaknesses are in the relationship in order to rebuild a higher level of connection that is individually satisfying.

I ask each of them to rate on a scale from 1-10 – 10 being completely satisfied and 1 being not satisfied – each of the six categories. For example, let's take Gregg and Maureen. They both claim they would score the need for Security within the relationship as being met at a nine. Awesome! Gregg gives Variety a two and Maureen, a three. Ugh. Significance a three by Gregg and one by Maureen – ugh again – while love is scored a seven by both. Pretty good! The last two categories are what Robbins calls the Spirit Needs. When those needs are being met, the relationship is growing, and so are your purposes, individually or collectively. I do not even address this with a couple until we can get the Personality ones at decent levels. Eight and up is ideal while a six or seven can be "enough" but won't give you that Rockstar relationship you are looking for. Typically of the four Personality Needs, we have two that are most important to us. Men I have found have a high need for Significance, while it's not unusual for a woman to have a high need for Love/Connection.

So what does this scoring tell me about Gregg and Maureen? It tells me that although they feel really secure in the other person the relationship is a bit boring or flat. It also tells me that both Maureen and Gregg are not feeling particularly appreciated or respected within the marriage, although deep down inside they "know" they are loved by their spouse. Now for most couples, especially ones that have been together for a very long time, this is a pretty typical scenario. Passion is gone. Relationship could possibly be near sexless. Both parties have gotten so complacent that they take each other for granted which often leads to looking for significance primarily outside the marriage. This doesn't necessarily mean infidelity, although it can. Significance can be found in the workplace, the community, same-sex friendships, their children, or even their place of worship :-). In and of themselves, these are respectable ways of getting emotional needs met, but can often result in much distance between the partners with long hours away or living very separate lives. I see these as ways to exit the marriage emotionally without physically leaving. Same diff to me ... we're there in body but not in spirit. It's like a person's soul leaving their body before their vitals actually shut down. Are they really still "there" or just a dead corpse? Lifeless. In my observation, this is a very culturally acceptable model of a marriage. Pretty status quo, I would even say. It worked for me for a long time. Some was a result of being married to a cop with a challenging schedule, but in the latter half, it was choosing to believe the lie, "This is as good as it gets," so I would not have to be faced with a decision to leave or stay. I personally have arrived at a point in my life where status quo is not negotiable. That's the point I'm trying to make here. *Why* settle? Are you not as deserving as anyone else of what life can give you abundantly? Okay, okay that's me. I'm a go-big or go-home kinda gal and do respect that every person decides for themselves what their standard will be. So if my words are physically causing your body to react, then *listen* to what it is trying to tell you. Take action. Choose: you and your partner can take your relationship with commitment and intention upward (assuming they are with you on this) or be honest, – heart level honest – whether there is too much hurt, mistrust, resentment, core differences, or a plain ol' uncaring attitude to lovingly support each other to meet these needs at a high level within the relationship.

In the case of Gregg and Maureen, they chose to take action as a couple and focus on bringing more feelings of Variety and Significance in their relationship.

They went about this by first revisiting activities where early in their relationship they experienced fun together. The years of responsibility with a home, children, and careers took all the fun out their marriage. They made a commitment to one another to carve out at least one time during the week to do a fun activity. This of course is subjective to every couple, so the only requirement is that you are experiencing fun together, free for a time of all responsibility in order to affirm as a couple you are still friends and enjoy each other's company. This computes to the brain as positive reinforcement that the relationship is meeting the need for Variety. Of course, consistency is crucial to reintegrate a previous pattern in the relationship in order to erase the old belief.

The other need they collaborated on was Significance. The years had also diluted the appreciation they had for one another. Each was caught up in their own to-do list of life which caused them to no longer be aware of how the other was serving them and their life. Gregg and Maureen began an early morning ritual before work to spend time in gratitude of the other. It could either be in service – like bringing them coffee in bed – or verbally sharing before starting the day what they appreciated or valued in the other from the previous day. This activity alone performed consistently in less than three minutes a day sent the relationship to a whole new level of positivity. Because of their love and commitment to one another, the couple made it a priority to cultivate their marriage regularly in these needs.

This is one of the ways we cherish our partner – by feeding and nurturing each other's needs within the partnership and exhibiting that it has value to us. Their marriage moved on to flourish from just these two small consistent shifts and they received a much higher level of fulfillment from it than before we began our sessions.

But what if we took the opposite case? Sometimes by the time one of the parties thinks enough is enough, many years of hurt and betrayal have taken the wind out of their sails. On a head level (ego) they want to try but on a heart level (spirit), they have either gone numb or lost desire.

So what I am proposing here? The same unbelievably hard decision I put in my own face. How dare I hold another person captive for my own selfish needs for security, whether it be financial or emotional, or just because I am too much of a coward to face my fear of the unknown. In my own case, it was primarily the latter. What I see in my office often is that both parties know the relationship is in serious trouble. They are drowning in some sort of unhealthy cycle, whether they admit it to themselves or not. In my own marriage I was the one to call bullcrap. Bullcrap on the reality of the years of hurt, betrayal, abandonment, and selfishness on both our parts. Remember, infidelity does not only come in the form of sexual unfaithfulness. Anytime we choose to ignore our partner's needs for certainty, variety, significance, or love, the other person feels on some level betrayal or abandonment. Men seem to have trouble really getting this concept. This is mostly due to the fact that culturally we are thinking in too black and white terms.

Let me give you an example of another couple, Dan and Winnie. Dan has a passion for football. Of course, he's obsessed with watching the NFL (maybe sometimes even betting on them in a pool). Dan will sit for hours, whether in his man cave or at a bar with his buddies, watching college as well. Dan and Winnie have a three- and a half-year-old and a new baby and recently moved into a new home. Needless to say, responsibilities have increased greatly. On the weekends, Winnie has certain expectations of Dan to help around the house and give her a break from the kids. During the week, Dan consistently promises to step up and carry his load of the couple's responsibilities, whether it be to the home or his family. But somehow when the weekend does come, his love of football wins out. He makes some excuse that it's an important game or a buddy he hasn't seen in a while, or he had a rough week so "I deserve this time." Week after week, month after month, or even year after year, Dan's word is no longer his word. Winnie no longer trusts his word. Long-term patterns of this in a marriage, which many people will minimize, will cause significant damage. This is what I call cumulative injury. Consistent repetition of small "cuts" leads to resentment and distancing. In relation to the Six Core Human Needs, Winnie's need for connection is compromised because she no longer feels Dan is her partner (teammate). She cannot count on him.

So just to be fair (because I despise double standards!), let's reverse this. Let's take another couple I've worked with, Kevin and Maggie. They too have two children about ages nine and twelve. Both children are involved, as many kids today, in numerous extracurricular activities. Kevin works a nine-to-five job as a computer programmer and Maggie as a school teacher. After work, Maggie rushes home to grab the kids to get them to their respective activities, returning home anywhere between five to seven where Kevin has already started dinner or picked something up. Dinner is swallowed whole while kids are off to do homework, bathe, and go to bed. Maggie does her lesson plans for the next day and then proceeds to hop on social media or call her girlfriends until it's time for bed. Kevin asks her to please put down her phone down and spend some intimate time with him. There's always some excuse though with Maggie. She needs her down time or has to return some calls promising again and again "tomorrow night honey." Kevin begins to withdraw, tired of the constant disappointment or maybe even, sense of rejection. He feels very insignificant to Maggie. His Core Need to feel significant to her is not being met. He too begins to find her words empty.

I used these two examples because most people tend to only think the big things destroy a marriage – abuse, addiction, or adultery – which they do, but what I just exemplified is the "slow death" of a relationship until one day you wake up and you wonder why you feel the way you do. Empty, unfulfilled, not going anywhere. It's bit perplexing to some because it's not like they are a bad person or abusive … maybe just neglectful or self-absorbed.

So if your relationship is on this slippery slope of descending apathy, I suggest strongly that the two of you sit down and evaluate it from these six needs and see where the foundation is weak. Collectively discuss an action plan as a couple to improve the low-scoring needs. Again, I cannot stress enough that this is a shift in how you show up in the relationship **consistently**! Just as on New Year's, when we commit to change our eating and exercise habits to transform our bodies, we do the same within our relationships. Otherwise, you will find yourself right back in that emotional heaviness – similar to regaining body weight if we don't follow a regular lifestyle plan. This concept is crucial to a thriving marriage.

Cultivate it to grow it and keep it alive. Sorry men – a "wham-bam-thank-you-ma'am" attitude is not going to work here.

My hope is to awaken you to the reality that there are very insidious ways to exit a marriage emotionally in contrast to the more obvious. It all ends up in the same place: emotional distance and disconnection. Your spirit feels dead and so does the relationship.

In the next chapter, I'll share how to make your wants or needs crystal clear to your partner so you can mutually co-create the rockstar relationship you've been dreaming of!

Chapter Six

Getting Clear

"If you don't set a baseline standard for what you'll accept in life, you'll find it's easy to slip into behaviors and attitudes or a quality of life that's far below what you deserve."

–Anthony Robbins

I tend to be an eclectic person. If you saw my home, you would know that. I've never been super matchy-matchy in decorating or my style of dress, either. The same applies to my therapeutic and coaching styles. I have been particularly drawn to the Law of Attraction and other universal laws. Intuitively, I have accomplished many of my goals by implementing some of these basic principles. Several years ago, I decided to take a more in-depth training to use this law more intentionally ... probably because my dreams were getting bigger! Anyhoo, one of the best principles I learned from it was the importance – and I mean vital importance – of getting clear on what you want – in life and specifically your health, career, finances, your spirituality, and your relationships. By learning this sorting process of getting clear on what I wanted and what I didn't want, I realized how many things I subconsciously was ambivalent about. If you don't know LOA, a key factor of it is the Universe gives you back exactly what you put out. Like attracts like. An analogy I often use is, if I was at a restaurant hemming and hawing about what to order, the server would stand there until he or she was clear on what I wanted. He would want to get the order right! Same goes for the Universe … "Ask and it is given." (BTW, a great book on LOA by Esther Hicks.) So what I am leading to here is two-fold. One is getting clear on what you do and don't want in your marriage … the more crystal clear, the better. Second, develop communication skills to convey that truth to your partner.

Quite often when I ask a client "What do you want?" possibly because I am meeting them at a time of confusion, they typically respond with "I'm not sure."

Okay, I get it – especially if they have been in long-term marriage where they have basically gone into a trance. So I have few tools I share with them to get the juices flowing.

I. **Start with getting clear on what you don't want.**

Sometimes once we clear out those items, what we *do* want becomes more apparent.

II. **A heart meditation/exploration.**

Sit with your eyes closed and breathe for several minutes into your heart center. Actually visualize the breath going in and out of the heart. Ask the question to yourself, "What do I want and *why*?" Don't go into your head! Stay in your heart and trust what arises. Notice how you feel at the hope of having this desire. The feeling is the clue to your wants.

III. **Muscle test.**

Remember what I said earlier about the body doesn't lie? Often we think we want something based on others' values or beliefs placed on us. Where to live? What career? Stay single or marry? Etc. Muscle testing is a method of using the body's intelligence to bring to our awareness what is truly our desire or for our best interest. There are many ways to muscle test. YouTube has tons of tutorials to learn muscle testing methods. Choose what feels most comfortable to you.

As you begin to get clearer (in your body) about what you want and what you don't want within the relationship, write those desires down with no ambiguity. In other words, "I am clear I no longer will accept a double standard within our relationship." Or "I am clear that I want all matters concerning the children to be mutually decided upon." And so on.

The second half of this step is verbally communicate it to your spouse in plain English. Now this may seem pretty elementary but I am utterly amazed at how adults have not acquired this skill within their marriages! Even couples that have been together for a considerable length of time – OMG! I'm not a huge public activist (but maybe now I am ;-)) but if there was any curriculum I would advocate to be in the high schools, it would be the Art of Assertiveness. Many people I encounter do not even know what assertiveness looks like! It's that place between passive and aggressive. Communicating clearly and respectfully. I cannot tell you how many marriages get into trouble because they do not know this skill efficiently. It seems simple, but people have great difficulty with acquiring this gentle but direct communication. Probably due to poor modeling as a child. Lordy be, I could go on about this. But seriously, how can it be that the person you have chosen to commit your heart to knows so little about your wants or don't-wants? I've heard it *all* from couples. Excuses like "I don't want to hurt their feelings." "He or she will get angry with me." "I'm afraid if I say what I really mean, I won't be able to stop." Oh, for Pete's sake, we are adults. I get it with your boss, or your in-laws, or neighbor, but your intimate partner not only should know your heart but needs to know it for your relationship to be real and thriving! Jesus taught "Speak the truth in love." Yep, that simple. Say what you need to say to get your point across from a heart motivation of love. Words of blame or attack are unnecessary and actually cause the other person to go into defense mode which leads to emotional deafness. In other words, you are sharing these wants or don't-wants not to divide but from a place of love. Your aim is not only to bring greater understanding to your partner but to speak from a place of loving yourself enough to make your boundaries and desires *known*. All that BS about "if he really loved me, he would know" is just that: BS. Say what you mean and mean what you say without intentionally damaging the other person's soul. The gift of this process is not only will your partner feel respected and honored by your kind communication, but you will feel equally as good about yourself and your ability to work through differences like an adult. This is actually how healthy conflict resolution can strengthen your bond and not weaken it through unnecessary mudslinging.

I suggest once you have a "come-to-Jesus" chat with your spouse that you ask them if they need any clarification to be clear themselves on what you are sharing. Often advising they end the conversation lovingly with "So are you clear?" It's amazing how we can think we are clear but our partner hears it so differently. Utterly amazing but oh so common.

Finding clarity and setting boundaries in your relationship is a necessary process for your relationship to thrive. It exhibits self-love and contributes greatly to reducing conflict in your marriages. At the root of most – if not all conflicts – is unmet expectations. So by putting them in plain English and allowing the other person to clarify what they heard is crucial but not the end of this process.

The beauty about humans is we have free will. We *do* have the power of choice. I think sometimes as adults our reptilian brain kicks in when presented with a request. Maybe it's that parent we can't say no to or that desperate need for approval from peers. No matter what the reason, we always have an option to deny the request. Always. -I wish I had a dollar for every time someone said to me "But you don't understand. I don't have a choice!" Wrong! What you are actually saying is you *do not like* your choices. Sometimes either we have created or allowed (same diff) our lives to get to such an uncomfortable point that in order to create change, our options are less than desirable. Change is not always easy but when it leads in a direction that is in integrity to yourself, it will always be worth the discomfort.

Of course sometimes we are the ones hearing "no." Hmmmmmmm, maybe that puts the ball back in our court. Let me use a more extreme example. Suppose Henry has a severe drinking problem. He manages to make it to work every day but stops for drinks with co-workers on the way home, missing dinner with his family. Then proceeds to plop himself on the couch where he continues to drink until he passes out. His wife feels abandoned and alone, not only in the marriage but with raising the kids. Weekends are worse. Finally Sandy finds the strength through attending her FA meetings to draw a hard line with Henry. She requests that he sober up and begin a twelve-step program with a sponsor in order for her to stay in the marriage. Henry says he will "cut back" but not eliminate it altogether. He says drinks after work help him to decompress from a stressful day and creates camaraderie amongst his team members. Sandy is done. It's all or nothing. She cannot live this way anymore. Sandy has a tough choice. Really tough choice. But she still has a choice. This unfortunately is where it gets complicated. It may feel like she's stuck, but she's not. She is choosing to stay stuck by not making a choice.

Choice is self-empowerment.

I see this scenario quite often in my practice when working with couples. When they first come in, their hope is that they want to coerce the other to change and change for good. Natural, right? Then they won't be stuck with difficult decisions. But in Sandy's case, where Henry stated his "bottom line," her work was to become strong enough to make a choice that would be in integrity to the life she wanted and deserved. It's the pain that Sandy is trying to avoid. Sorry, not possible. Does she move through short-term pain for long-term gain, or just stay in what she already knows – and Henry has made clear by his choice – will be long-term pain? Sandy with my guidance needed to see she was empowered to choose. She was not a victim to Henry's choice to continue drinking. I worked with her until she felt more empowered by her options ... until she saw for herself her power in choice. Going inward and connecting to all the untapped resources within her gave her the ability to leave her marriage and eventually find a relationship that cherishes her soul.

Probably another topic that should be taught in school curriculums! Self-empowerment. Again I am not saying her choice was easy – but it was still there.

You may be able to identify a boundary or even put it out there. But keeping it on a consistent basis, especially after long term patterns of undefined or unclear boundaries, can be quite the challenge to stay committed to. The F word creeps up again: *fear.* Boundaries were definitely something that were very weak in my marriage on both sides. Again things not taught in school! *Aaaaaaaargh.* Ignorant and naive patterns befall the best of us until someone wakes up and calls BS. But sometimes neither one wakes up and both people drag each other down into a life that is far from what they desire, deserve, and is certainly light years away from its fullest potential. This can tragically result in two wasted lives when the decision to split has a greater chance of not only saving one life but possibly two.

Now again, this was an extreme example but the energy underneath is just the same as if Sandy was a hoarder and Henry had it up to his eyeballs. Again more acceptable in society? More aaaaaaaaargh….

In the next chapter, we are going to hit emotional boot camp to dig deep to the roots of these patterns that feel like the undertow is too great to break free from.

There is no growth in the comfort zone and no comfort in the growth zone. You have a choice!

CHAPTER SEVEN

Dig Deep

"He who looks outside, dreams. He who looks inside, awakes."

–Carl Jung

I'm a personal growth junkie. I admit it! As I said earlier, for as long as I can remember, I have been trying to figure what this whole thing called life is about. We had a beautiful weeping willow tree in the side yard of the house I grew up in. One of my fondest memories of childhood was sitting under that tree on a summer afternoon. Aaaaaaah the breeze and the shading of the overhanging branches blowing felt so freeing. It wasn't just cooling, it was soothing. I'm sure it was a way that I also calmed my anxiety as a child from my inconsistent and tumultuous home life. I can remember looking to the sky and my thoughts drifting to all the big questions like: "Where was I before this? Where is heaven? Where is God?" It felt more spiritual than emotional but then the two became entwined.

By the time I hit 30, I had been in and out of therapy quite a bit, primarily because of a deep depression that I fell into right after I got married that melded into a low-spectrum eating disorder. But nonetheless, in my usual fashion, I needed to know the "whys" of my behavior and attitudes. Bigger marital problems began to develop right after the birth of my second daughter so I continued to stay in therapy individually and with my spouse. Unfortunately, he had quite the high maintenance and controlling mother whose personality brought very challenging issues to our marriage. Rick had much difficulty saying no to her or putting my requests before hers and it resulted in me almost constantly feeling second to her. I could probably go into a rant of stories about that dynamic but I think you get the idea. It was a huge factor in not feeling cherished in the relationship that Rick was never able to fully grasp.

All in all, I still found my struggles to be gifts. Maybe not immediately, but once I began to go underneath I could see that they were all God-given opportunities to grow and so life became my classroom. During these years, my father passed and my slightly older brother battled with an aggressive AIDS virus that took his life at 37. Life by age 34 was hitting me full force. But through each challenge, I was learning to lean into the pain a little bit more and using it to grow deeper in my faith and as a person. I began again to use my empty marriage as a place of learning and eventually, recovery from a long-time pattern of not cherishing myself. I feel fortunate that for whatever reason I was equipped with that resiliency. Not everyone is. Look around – we can find people everywhere that see life as against them instead of for them. That's a dangerous perspective that can suck you into a vortex of victimization for life! Besides discomfort, one of the other major reasons I went to therapy or dug deep into my own psyche is because I believe every marriage is a co-creation. It is never – and I repeat never – only one-sided. How do we confirm that? Because remember we always have a choice. One's partner's behavior could have more severe consequences or damage to the relationship but even the so-called victim has a part in the state of the relationship. In my situation, I felt we both did our fair share of our demise by commission and also by omission or passivity. So to me, the only way I could get clear was to tease out what was *my* stuff to own and what was *his*. My journey and experience has given me the tools and expertise to aid you through your own discovery with clarity so you can get to living your life with passion and purpose!

Childhood wounding and conditioning can run deep. But it's all on a spectrum. These patterns don't break easily because there are usually layers and layers of these beliefs held in our body even on a cellular level. That was what I was unaware of at that time. I definitely was working on the cognitive/behavioral while integrating my spirituality and for a while, there was surviving with occasional moments of soaring but they wouldn't last long. It got me "through" many more years. I was often told by husband that I had too high of expectations or was too idealistic in relationships and for a while … a long while, I believed it. You see, when something inside us is trying to get our attention whether it's a desire for real love or a dream to pursue, it will be relentless until we finally take action. Cycles/patterns are very common not only in relationships but through all areas of our life. We continue to be creatures of habit, although not always ones that are in our best interest.

Lo and behold, this theme in my marriage kept circling around. "Why does it feel so disconnected?" "I know he loves me but I can't feel it." I literally felt this hole in my heart that was desiring connection to bring breath to life. I yearned for it terribly. I wanted a life of meaning and depth and a partner who understood and supported it. There were times when I wanted to retreat from everyone and everything – times when my bed and the television felt a very safe place to ride out the rest of my years. But I would always circle around after a time and get a second wind. I feel blessed to return to the inertia within because it kept prodding me forward on my path to find me again.

Besides our conditioning, I have also come up with the theory that people in long-term marriages – especially ones that started in high school or even early college years – have their own type of conditioning as well. The lack of certain emotional awareness or the desire to escape a painful home environment thrust many of us into early marriages in the hope to rescue ourselves. In other words, marriage becomes an extension or continuance of our childhood wounding unless we can wake up from this lifelong trance.

In my practice, I have found my advanced training in heart-centered hypnotherapy to be my most powerful modality to break co-dependent patterns. This process has an amazing way of lifting the smoke screen from the distortions we often carry. I came across this modality when I returned to mainstream counseling once again to try and figure out what was "wrong with me." I'd been scratching my head constantly saying it *must* be all me. Pretty much what all experienced co-dependents say! I knew if I was going to get to the bottom of things, I had to get to the root cause. I "knew" – because of my previous dabbling with the subconscious – that it was where I needed to get to. Again checking in with my heart, I followed this path not only to do my own healing but to further my effectiveness with my clients. I was tired of Band-Aids and short-term fixes. I wanted healing and I wanted to offer my clients the same. Best choice I ever made thus far in my career – and I am beyond grateful for the teaching I received through the Wellness Institute in Seattle, WA.

I was relentless in this process, determined to not only find more clarity whether my marriage was over but to return back to who I once was. Talk about exhilarating! Wow! I was beyond done going around the same block not only in my marriage but within myself.

I would not say you would have to do all the things that are in my "dig deep boot camp" but a combination of these modalities would be helpful in getting to the truth of your heart. The truth of *you*. The beauty of you so you can cherish yourself in order to allow another to do the same.

Below is a list of the modalities I would encourage you to research for self- healing and awareness or to find local practitioners to work with you. I use the best and most appropriate of these in my practice when I work with a client and personally have implemented them in my own healing process on an ongoing basis to clear negative thought patterns.

Here is the list:
- Heart-Centered Hypnotherapy
- Essential Oils
- Reiki
- EFT/Tapping
- Creative Visualization
- Meditation
- Subliminals
- Journaling
- Yoga
- Therapeutic Massage
- Breathwork Therapy
- Myofascial Release

These are the ones I personally experienced and that worked very well for me in my transformation.

Just like any military training, "dig deep boot camp" requires commitment to yourself, the process, and to knowing that not changing is *no longer* an option. Good intentions, hope, and half-hearted attempts to rewire thought patterns or behaviors is not commitment. Commitment to change only happens when going backward or remaining where you are is non-negotiable.

Any good therapist knows we do not get anyone to change nor do our clients get people in their life (i.e. spouse) to change. It is nothing short of arrogance if either one thinks we are that powerful. What brings change into our lives is stepping into our own power. Realizing the Divine power that is within us to transform, morph, or create. Digging deep into our hearts, souls, and psyches to find that power we lost or most likely gave away a long time ago takes courage. It takes vision and it takes not only self-love but also love for others.

Everything in life is a ripple effect. The further I went on my path of evolution, the more I saw my inability to change people I encounter. But what I did see was the power I have to influence those I cross paths with and those I love. To inspire or give permission to others to go for what they truly want in their lives.

Everything is energy: every action, every word, every thought that moves from us creates a ripple effect. Do not underestimate your power to influence others!

So whether you do something great in this world or not, your energy is your contribution to this world and in this case, your relationship.

Relationships can be hard. Sometimes real hard. But they don't have to be except for this thing called our ego that loves to prove, protect, and preserve – not the relationship but ourselves! Love, if we are truly loving, connects, includes, and expands. This again is one of those simple principles that is so difficult (at least to me) to implement. Oh, I thought compared to the average person that I was pretty decent at loving. Sadly, a majority of couples I work with abide by the system of "I'll give when I get." What is the basis of that model? Fear. We are in protection of our hearts. I get it. For sure I get it. And maybe at times we feel it's necessary or warranted … and maybe at times it is. But I can promise you no relationship will thrive in that atmosphere, and we will never ever get the love we want if we are that guarded. A shield is a shield. If we put that there to protect us from pain then by default it keeps us from love.

Oh no we don't think that consciously! But this is why self-evaluation is key in a thriving relationship. Self-honesty is crucial. As a therapist I would never expect my clients to walk a path I was unwilling. How dare we expect another person to give to us what we are unwillingly to give? I mean how many times have we heard "Do unto others as we would want done unto us?" OMG world, wake up! This one principle, if we really, not half-heartedly, applied it with as much integrity as humanly possible could change the state of the entire world. But change happens in smaller arenas before more globally so it makes sense the consciousness of the world will not change until we can get this in our family systems first. This is all spiritual truth no matter what religion you practice. But until we stop letting ego dominate our relationships as it proves, protects, and preserves our turf, we will be like a two-handled saw in a back and forth pattern, deepening the groove in the wood until it divides in two.

Superior evaluation can create superior results within our personal development and our relationships. This again my friend is not easy but oh so gratifying if you want to more than just "get through" this life. I've walked this path and will continue to because just surviving is not an option for me. A shallow, disconnected, and flat union to me is not acceptable if I am going to live my life to the fullest. I definitely took the long way home with lots of cuts, bruises, and scars but I would not trade this journey for anything for I am alive!

CHAPTER EIGHT

Walking the Talking

*"You might think she wants your car, money or gifts ...
but the right woman wants your time, your smile, your
honesty, your effort, and your willingness to make her
a priority."*

–Charles Orlando

One of the most destructive thought patterns I come across consistently is a victim mentality. I admit I have fallen prey to it off and on through my life. Oh, I still do! But now maybe it will last an hour or at most a day (we all deserve a little pity party) rather than as years ago when I stayed in it for days, weeks, months, or even years! Thankfully I always would pull out of it.

Another term for victim mentality is learned helplessness. Very toxic! Why? Because there is a core belief deep inside that believes you have no way out of a feeling, situation, or circumstance. A core belief that was most likely imprinted at a very young age and became your default mode when things got too difficult in life.

Another way of looking at this is that we can feel powerless over our life or circumstances. I suppose you could look at the world that way. I mean, we can't change the weather, traffic, or people or – in this case our partner.

It is not going to serve you to get clear if your marriage is sputtering out and you feel you have no options but to accept it as how it "has to be". This thinking could be a significant hindrance if your challenges in your relationship have become so acute that you feel there is no waking your man up.

As I mentioned earlier, I love to implement principles of LOA both with my clients and in my personal life. So let me ask you … have you ever had a vision for your relationship? I mean an intentional, clear vision. If you have, kudos to you but I actually have never met a couple who uses this tool.

Communication is often a very weak factor in relationships in trouble. Having a vision for your relationship is a "part" of having effective communication.

Visualization is an *extremely* powerful tool in *anything* you want to accomplish in life. One of my personal favorite Law of Attraction tools in couples' work is a vision board. In short a vision board is collage of pictures and words that represent the abundance you desire to create in life. In this case, as a couple. Abundance not only in the area of finances, but health, personal growth, spirituality, philanthropic or leisure.

It is not uncommon when coaching a couple to hit areas of "style" differences. For example recently I was working with a couple named Lisa and Artie. Lisa was your typical type A, go-getter, planner, and incessant list maker. Artie liked to structure his life somewhat loosely. This was often a huge point of contention between the couple. Artie perceived Lisa as a bit neurotic and controlling while Lisa thought Artie was non-committal to any "plan" and never able to make a clear cut decision on just about everything which often left her feeling frustrated and anxious. Their individual "style" of approaching outcomes was polar opposite. I explained to Artie some key universal points in how the science of LOA is effective in creating what you desire in life.

My explanation of how this universal law works seemed to quell his need for the exercise to "make sense". One definition of the word "cherish" is to "keep a hope and ambition in one's mind." By having Artie and Lisa create a vision board together it was not only a way to blend their styles of obtaining goals but also a way of cherishing each other's dreams. Valuing and nurturing each other's dreams without putting one above the others in addition to fostering together their joint desires.

Prior to this Lisa thought that Artie was not supporting or upholding in her dreams or goals by taking a more "we'll-figure-it-out-as-we-go" approach. This certainly did not make her feel cherished! Through the process of creating a vision board they were able to share, discuss, support, and dream their future together in the container of a "loosely structured" modality. Delightfully a win-win outcome.

Men who have difficulty understanding a woman's need to be cherished lack emotional intelligence. I get usually not a big part of this conditioning although my intention is to bring more awareness to them through my future writings. But the fact is guys that get the most quality sex in their relationship are the ones who know a woman's heart. Call him a wuss or whatever, he's getting laid and I'll bet the ones who are still Neanderthals are not. Just sayin'....

There are several factors that can lead to the death of a marriage but this one factor in particular is connected to the bedroom. My experience is the more a woman feels not only loved but truly *cherished* the more she will open herself to her man.

I'm not a man hater ... in fact, I'm in love with one. But man oh man, this where I have seen and still see so many guys miss the mark. Clearly, I am a baby boomer who is not bound by certain antiquated traditions but this is not what I'm exactly saying. Sure, I still think chivalry is sexy. Absolutely. But I am not opposed to the woman taking the lead at times especially if a particular area is a strength for her. But it doesn't mean the man sloughs it off onto her indefinitely because she is "good at it." That's a cop out, plain and simple. We have all heard it before – we give time and attention to what we value-that's what cherishing is. When a woman is longing to be seen, valued, and delighted in, and she sees her husband year after year give more time and attention to planning his next fishing trip or detailing every nook and cranny of his motorcycle and then failing to give as much detail to what is "supposed to be" the love of his life then what she experiences in her body is that you're a liar. Don't say beautiful things in cards, texts, or in your words to get sex and not follow through with action.

Women are intuitive, feeling creatures. At first, we believe the words until something doesn't "feel" right. Then we start to notice the incongruence. I did but it took a while. A long while. Actually I liken it to being in a trance. Our mind is nodding yes while everything in our body is feeling a negative emotion. I believe it starts as hurt but after years or decades turns into anger, resentment, then contempt. If either party hits contempt, it's stage four cancer for the relationship. Anger in any form will always block connection. Contempt is the polar opposite of cherishing. And don't kid yourself into thinking your spouse can't feel that even if you don't utter a word! Oh sure, you can still go through the motions of sex but connection, true, soulful connection is impossible while that wall of anger exists.

Approaching or existing in a marriage in a very cerebral way can contribute to a woman feeling confused. I know I felt this way repeatedly in my marriage. I have female clients that have come in with all the following statements:

- I mean yeah, he doesn't plan dates but he really is a good guy.

- But he does work hard at work and so I can't be upset he didn't plan something for my birthday.
- He always kisses me goodbye in the morning and says I love you.
- Overall, he's a good guy. He rarely gets angry, let's me do my own thing and never complains about much.
- Well, at least he did "something"....

In each statement what are they all doing? Denying their heart. Their heart is broken that their man remembers them with an afterthought. Ouch.

Actually in many cases, he is just being a guy, albeit still checked out and insensitive. If you want your relationship to move from just surviving to thriving, you must be able to find a way to communicate to your man how your heart *feels*.

The best example I use is a car. I find most men can relate to this analogy. I say: "Suppose you just bought the car of your dreams. How would you take care of it? Listening to it for sure! Checking out the squeaking, sputtering, clunking to determine if it's trying to communicate that there is an issue. Would you ignore that issue day after day, week after week, month after month, and hopefully not year after year! Most likely not because it will go kaput before that. Now thankfully human beings are a bit more durable than a car but I think you get the point. Yes?"

What I am trying to get at is gaining clarity not only of your wants and needs but of the relationship. I am trying to help you determine whether first you have clearly communicated your wants and needs assertively. Secondly, when the two of you are coming at the relationship from two different angles, is he able to meet you halfway in anything to show how loved, valued, and cherished you truly are?

I can't say I've researched this, but have observed this in my office or life's classroom but some men are handicapped in emotional intelligence. I have self-researched and come to some conclusions about "why" but that is not of consequence right now. But what I will say is use some of the methods I discussed earlier in the book to clear the path to your heart. Work on trusting your heart as to whether there is the ability to create that connected, soulful, and fluid relationship where being cherished is what keeps it alive. Be scrupulous in your assessment of your relationship. Be *soulfully* honest to yourself and your partner about your wants and needs. Your vision. Your blueprint. It is only then you will have the clarity to see things as they truly are and decide which direction is most honoring to yourself and your partner.

CHAPTER NINE

Soul to Soul

*"Be impeccable with your word. Speak with integrity.
Say only what you mean…Use the power of your word
in the direction of truth and love."*

–Don Miguel Ruiz

One of my favorite lines from the movie *A Few Good Men* is when Tom Cruise insists on the truth from Jack Nicholson. And he replies with "You can't handle the truth." When I saw that movie back in the day the impact of that line did not have near the relevance that it does now. The very first vision board I ever did back in 1998, I put a bright light smack dab in the center and cut out the letters T R U T H to put below it. Sometimes we forget what we ask for; we may not even be aware we asked for some things. A prayer to me is a desire of the heart, audible or not. In Universal terms, an intention. We are sending intentions with every thought we have. Thoughts emit energy just like a light bulb emits light! Positive or negative – I believe the ones we hold in commitment to ourselves always show up. I came to realize over the years since I created that vision board, which I see as a form of prayer or intention, that for many years I did not want to see certain truths either about myself, my husband, or the marriage.

The hardest thing about being boldly honest with ourselves is then we will have to live in the angst of knowing we need to do something about what we see in our situation or self. Denial is a powerful coping mechanism.

It protects from what we are unwilling to see because we believe we are not capable of handling the reality of it. It's ego. It protects and preserves us. The truth sometimes is brutally painful to see whether it's a loss of a loved one, diagnosis of a terminal disease, or owning the reality of another person's abusive behavior to us. Honestly, the most challenging piece of my own transformation process has been owning the truth about myself (i.e. shadow parts) and how that has caused damage to another person. So if you choose to take this road less traveled, I must precaution you that the self-evaluation or purging can be brutal but necessary. Of course, that will vary from person to person. I had some behavior that clearly caused others much pain and I had to own that first in order to free myself to move forward into a life that was congruent with my authentic self. Not to mention the anger and unforgiveness toward myself for the years of giving away my power, not using my voice, and therefore throwing myself under the bus! I had to stop blaming others and realize I allowed all of it. That was the hardest pill to swallow. I chose to be the victim because I did not believe at the time that I had the power, courage, or strength within me to change things that were true but not okay with me.

I remember the first time I came across the famous quote by M. Williamson that held within it, "Our deepest fear is that we are powerful beyond measure." Wow did it resonate with me on a deep level and definitely everything in my body was saying yes. Yes, I am. My faith told me that too. On a day to day basis, I was able to absorb that and apply it in the smaller challenges of life. But believing that in the big challenges was a whole other thing.

Bob Proctor, a pioneer in the field of personal development, coined a phrase called the Terror Barrier. You can be sure when you step out of your comfort zone and attempt to do something you never thought you could or would that fear will show up. For me, it was terror as his theory suggests. Bob has a great video on YouTube that illustrates how this phenomenon occurs in our body when we are stepping out in faith into the unknown. It shows up as terror because our brain is reading it as a threat to our survival. Of course we are going to freak! I did. Many times. But by using the processes I mentioned in Chapter Seven, I was able to break through it and toward what I wanted for my life. Yep, and I didn't die. Gratifying, very, to now experience and know what power is available to me as a result my journey. It's within me, always was, and always will be.

I understand that your circumstances may look different than mine or anyone's who is considering or choosing to leave their marriage. I honor that. You should too. Travel this path with integrity, intention, and soulfulness. Navigate through your heart with the simple but wise words of the Serenity Prayer:

> God, grant me the serenity to accept the things I cannot change.
> Courage to change the things I can,
> And wisdom to know the difference.

We can want our spouse to change or be a certain way all we want. We can ask, bargain, manipulate, coerce, or even tantrum. All the antics in the world will not change the fact there will be characteristics, behaviors, or traits that only we can decide if we can accept and love without condition. Nagging, criticizing, withdrawing, judging the person we claim to love is soul slaughter.

I have regrets about using those methods to get Rick to be what I wanted or needed him to be for my liking. We all do it in our relationships so don't beat yourself up for it, just know it is not effective. Remember, I'm inviting you to be brutally honest with yourself. We all do it when we operate from fear. It's just what we do unconsciously to try and keep our selves safe. Control the outcome. I did for years. But I found my way out by freeing us both of the captivity we held each other in for our personal agendas. I am committed albeit not perfectly to a new way of being, moving forward in my life. I advocate here truth, hard truth to yourself and your partner. That is integrity a.k.a. being straight up!

I kind of chuckle here because what I'm saying is we should all be true to ourselves. How foreign! Our culture has operated opposingly for so long it seems either ludicrous or impossible to imagine what that might actually look like. So maybe it is lofty but I have found such a freedom in it that I want to share that possibility with others who sense the call.

In the end, it's your choice if you choose to create more authenticity and happiness in your life. Relationships come in all shapes, sizes, colors, and tones. You decide what is in alignment for your true self to emerge. You decide what is negotiable and non-negotiable within the dynamic of your marriage. You are the expert of you. No one else. The process I shared in this book is an effective framework to discover your inner voice and your audible one! What might be ok for you might not be to me. What you want from your relationship may look different than what I would desire. A lot of wiggle room for preference.

Then you can decide with clarity if you both can transform what you have into a thriving, growing relationship or, in love, free yourself into a life that cherishes who you are.

CHAPTER TEN

A New Face for Marriage

"Commitment is an act not a word."

–Jean Paul Sartre

I am one of those quirky people who will find meaning in almost anything. You know the Divine coincidences or synchronicity jargon. It is Easter Day that I am writing this final chapter. So of course I am contemplating why I am in my office today writing this conclusion. My daughters think I am a bit over the top reading into things too much. And maybe at times I am. Don't care – it has served me well most of the time and has often been my source of direction after prayer. In the Christian tradition in which I was raised and have spent much of my adult life, Easter is about New Life … rising again. Needless to say, I am pondering the fact that I am completing the final draft of this book on this day. I choose to believe there is Divine Guidance in these words I am about to share because they are not facts, research, or theology – simply me sharing my heart, my thoughts about marriage, and how it pertains to our lives.

I remember asking my ex-husband, shortly before I made my decision to first separate, what he believed was the purpose of marriage and this journey of life. Around that time we were both entrenched in a Christian community so it was not unusual to have discussions like this from a spiritual (religious) perspective. I cannot fully remember his answer but I know it was one of the conversations that gave me more clarity about why our relationship was "feeling" so heavy and exhausting. We were trying to pull the other one to our way of thinking! Miserable! If I recall correctly, from my perspective, Rick had more mainstream views of marriage and life while mine were expanding by the day!

I am not saying he was wrong and I was right or vice versa, but we were opposed on a fundamental perspective as to how to move forward within the marriage. It felt like we were traveling the road of life for many years with certain gaps in perspectives like the kids or money. Yet other times, we walked fairly congruently. What this impasse felt like to me was a fork in the road. My way or your way? This way or that way. I am well aware couples hit differences all the time; in this case, fundamentally to the core, it felt to me this was not a negotiation of whether we should retire to Florida or the Carolinas. This felt very different. Do we stay together and appease one or the other to make life more comfortable for us and our family – or do we step risk the fear to continue on our souls' journey. I diligently remained committed to gaining clarity on which way to go. I discovered I "knew" that it was time to part ways. For me, my soul required it.

What do I believe the purpose of marriage is, now, standing where I am versus age 21? Growth. Growth and more growth. Transformation is uncomfortable, whether it's spiritual, emotional, or physical. But it's necessary for our growth and evolution. At a minimum, discomfort is required for the evolution of soul. In Christianity, we would say, "More like Christ." I agree wholeheartedly. I think I was drawn to study the Bible because it was filled with examples of kings, prophets, or followers of Jesus who took numerous wrong turns before their souls were truly awakened. I found comfort in that as I navigated through a marriage that I knew was not in integrity. No one's path is ever perfect. In fact, I know it was because of my mistakes, the mistakes of others, and my challenges that I am where I am as I sit and write this on Easter Day.

Like I said, since very early childhood, I have sensed a pull toward the spiritual path. That has never really waned in my life, in spite of some poor choices. I'm human.

Whether we realize it or not, we are in almost constant battle between ego and spirit. Love or fear. Right or wrong. Good or evil. It's all the same thing!

I am not here to tell you what your marriage should or shouldn't be. I desire with all my heart for you to be in a relationship that cherishes all of you.

As a writer, I am here to share with you my soul's journey and lessons I've learned along the way. If it resonates, cool. If not, toss it. Those goosebumps, chills, and the emphatic yes from your heart is resonance. Alignment with your own soul.

Knowledge is something we learn through books and education. Wisdom we acquire through experience. They are very different. Being somewhat rebellious to mainstream education, I have typically valued wisdom far more than education. I know I wanted the same for my daughters but then I realized by protecting them from pain in their lives I was actually robbing them of wisdom.

I got sucked into the Illusion of the world. I was completely fooling myself that by playing the game I would somehow hide from them the truth of life. Truth is felt. So hide all your defects from your children – your thoughts, your demons, your addictions – it won't matter because it's all felt, absorbed, or inherited because it's still alive and is energy. Toxic energy like carbon monoxide. Don't kid yourself – it is in the home you live in, no matter how pretty or perfect. No matter how many awards, As or accolades you have, your family feels that suppressed hidden energy in your home and marriage like cancer.

This was the awakening I had. Prior to that, I was not in a marriage to evolve, grow, or be enlightened. Heck no, I was still caught in the matrix of the system. The phrase "you can run but you can't hide" never resonated so perfectly for me until I saw this reality. I could not hide any longer behind the American dream life I had created. And most importantly, it was for me completely wrong to keep duping myself, my spouse, and family that I was happy. Love to me was no longer controlling or creating outcomes but being true to myself and trusting that an Organic Flow would prod Rick and my daughters into the evolution of their souls.

So what is my view of marriage today from where I am sitting at this moment in time? First of all, "traditional" marriages are no longer serving many individuals well. Primarily women. Women no longer need to sit at the feet of a man to ask him to take care of them in exchange for food and shelter. Survival is no longer based on a legal union. Women have choices like never before and have the same opportunities as men to advance themselves in any field. But to me that's all man-made BS. Sure legalities in a union afford people certain societal benefits that single people are not afforded. Fine, it's what sometimes we need to do to make our lives easier or to be accepted in certain arenas. Personal choice. I respect it. But again in my opinion, the real reason we even came into this world was for us to grow spiritually. Period. Spiritual beings having a human experience.

I am often amused how both men and women seem to think that if we get a ring on a finger we are guaranteed security or that the other person can't go anywhere. Can't fault them. I naively fell prey to that too. At least it makes it more difficult to leave and that might actually be a good thing as the impulsive creatures that we are.

Yet marriage first and foremost starts in the heart – the origin of all our personal truth. I'm still not seeing the world completely getting on board with this although we are inching our way toward it. I could name dozens of ways we exit emotionally, leaving our spouse feeling unseen, unheard, unappreciated, unloved, and uncherished – infidelity is not the only way to abandon commitment. Presence is needed more than just sitting at a dinner table or accompanying you to an event. It's feeling that a person is committed to you on every level of your being. Partnering with you not only emotionally, but in my opinion, even more so spiritually. A spiritual marriage supports you in your healing, growth, and purpose and cheers you on to the best version of you. They are for you. They meet your needs in love not obligation, yet realize no one can be the entire source of all of another's needs. This partnership is approached with intention and purpose. They are as committed to their own growth as you are to your own. You are "equally yoked" in that neither one has to drag the other uphill. Although there will be conflict, the conflict is used for your evolution, not just to prove who's right or to gain control.

We need to feel connection because that is in integrity to God's design. Because it is what heals us. Connection is not physically living under the same roof, playing house. It's alive and runs deep into our hearts.

When we approach each other with open hearts, seeking to meet each other's needs, we can find ourselves not just loved but cherished. *This* I wish for you.

About the Author

Christina Vazquez (Zeman), MA, has had a life-long passion for personal growth that far exceeds any formal education. In the past two decades, she has become a practicing psychotherapist with advanced clinical training in heart-centered hypnotherapy from the Wellness Institute, as well as certifications in Reiki, EFT, and Law of Attraction coaching. Her consistent personal study of the "science of relationships" integrated with the spiritual aspects, creates a broad approach to healing marriage and committed unions.

Christina brings an authenticity to her work with clients as well as to her writing. She transformed her personal journey through the challenge of marriage into a classroom that brings understanding and hands-on experience to her coaching style – and brings results to her clients.

Christina is a mother of three beautiful adult daughters and also a grandmother of three.

She resides in the southwest suburbs of Chicago with her life partner Bruce and two dogs. In their spare time, Christina and Bruce share a passion for music and perform acoustic sets at local venues. The couple actively incorporates personal and spiritual growth within their committed relationship for the expression of their collective and individual purposes.

About Difference Press

Difference Press is the exclusive publishing arm of The Author Incubator, an educational company for entrepreneurs – including life coaches, healers, consultants, and community leaders – looking for a comprehensive solution to get their books written, published, and promoted. Its founder, Dr. Angela Lauria, has been bringing to life the literary ventures of hundreds of authors-in-transformation since 1994.

A boutique-style self-publishing service for clients of The Author Incubator, Difference Press boasts a fair and easy-to-understand profit structure, low-priced author copies, and author-friendly contract terms. Most importantly, all of our #incubatedauthors maintain ownership of their copyright at all times.

Let's Start a Movement with Your Message

In a market where hundreds of thousands of books are published every year and are never heard from again, The Author Incubator is different. Not only do all Difference Press books reach Amazon bestseller status, but all of our authors are actively changing lives and making a difference.

Since launching in 2013, we've served over 500 authors who came to us with an idea for a book and were able to write it and get it self-published in less than 6 months. In addition, more than 100 of those books were picked up by traditional publishers and are now available in book stores. We do this by selecting the highest quality and highest potential applicants for our future programs.

Our program doesn't only teach you how to write a book – our team of coaches, developmental editors, copy editors, art directors, and marketing experts incubate you from having a book idea to being a published, bestselling author, ensuring that the book you create can actually make a difference in the world. Then we give you the training you need to use your book to make the difference in the world, or to create a business out of serving your readers.

Are You Ready to Make a Difference?

You've seen other people make a difference with a book. Now it's your turn. If you are ready to stop watching and start taking massive action, go to http://theauthorincubator.com/apply/.

"Yes, I'm ready!"

Other Books by Difference Press

Multi-Unit Franchise Mastery: Transform Your One-Unit Franchise Job into a Multi-Unit Franchise Enterprise (Franchise Success Book 2) by Aicha Bascaro

Overcoming Love Addiction: Your Recovery Roadmap by Lace N'Jon Bentley

Ignite Your Truth: Set Your Soul on Fire by Christie Hayden

The Zen Money Map: Charge Your Worth, Pay Yourself First, and Fund Your Wildest Dreams by Liz Lajoie

Crohn's and Colitis Fix: 10 Week Plan for Reversing IBD Symptoms and Getting Rid of Fatigue by Inna Lukyanovsky

Unleash the Beast: Escape Corporate Life to Live Your Dream Life by Sonjia Lioness Mackey

I Should Be Married: Hope and Inspiration for Living Happily Ever After by Marla Openshaw

Careers in Nonprofits: The Nonprofit Leader's Guide to Attracting, Hiring, and Retaining Top Talent by Nurys Harrigan Pedersen

The Relationship Roadmap: The Spiritual Guidebook to Ditch the Uncertainty and Find Clarity in Your Marriage (The Roadmap Series) by Kelli Reese

Level Up: Power Practices for Spiritual Superabundance by Sophia Remolde

Slow Travel: Escape the Grind and Explore the World by Jennifer Myrick Sparks

Finding Ugly: Transform Your Worst Moment into Your Greatest Gift by Scott Sunderland

Confessions of a Controlaholic: Don't Destroy Your Second Marriage Too! by Alexandra Union

Post-Divorce Bliss: Ending Us and Finding Me by Jude Walsh

Real Success: Feel Accomplished and Find Fulfillment in the Modern World by Michelle Zawaski

Thank You

I have so much more to tell you about the juicy subject of relationships but was not able to share it all in this book! When a relationship works, life can be joyful, abundant, and satisfying – but when your relationships are in conflict, everything in your life can feel off-kilter.

I want so much for you as my reader to learn conflict resolution for partners that leads to greater commitment and appreciation of one another. So, as a free gift to you, go to my website, anextraordinarylife.org, where you can get the link to my video:

Conflict to Connection

where you can learn how to master the art of healthy conflict resolution to that leads to deeper connection and intimacy instead of distance and disconnection.

See you there!

Printed in the United States
By Bookmasters